A Snapshot of the World in 26 Essays

Bella Erakko

In celebration
of all the stories
we've heard (or lived),
that have enriched us

© 2017 ALL RIGHTS RESERVED BELLA BARBARA ERAKKO
ISBN -13: 978-1981370405

A to Z:
A Snapshot of the World in 26 Essays

Introduction

After I finished writing the book, *Elsie at Ebb Tide: Emerging From the Undertow of Alzheimer's,* I knew I would enter a hiatus — perhaps for a long time. After all, I had nothing to say. One year, then two, and finally three years passed and my keyboard basically became a dust catcher (rather than a dream catcher).

There are times in our lives when we live between things. We retire, but haven't established an interesting post-retirement life. We have an injury, an illness, something that stops us in our tracks. We are living in between-time.

I remember sensing this would be my fate as I neared the words *The End* of my manuscript. I also know, from life experience, how it feels.

I can see one shore slipping slowly away. I can't swim back. An irresistible force shoves me deeper into the waters of not knowing. And then I know I'll be there — stuck perhaps for a considerable time — until I see a new shore.

Well, I'm still waiting.

So one day I decided I might as well write … something. I decided to pick one word from every letter in the alphabet and write an essay about it. I had only one rule: I had to write it in one day. It didn't have to be polished, but it did have to be finished.

A well-known author, Natalie Goldberg, wrote a classic *Writing Down the Bones*. In it, she insisted writers should write every day.

I never followed that advice. If I didn't have anything to say, I didn't say it. So the following essays are the exception to the rule. *What do I have to say when I have nothing in particular to say?*

It feels like going to the beach looking for shells. The sand looks barren as you approach it from the parking lot. You can't see anything of merit except sand. But slowly a whole amazing world opens up.

I think of the many people I've talked to who say, "Oh, I don't have that interesting a life." But then the conversation veers this way and that, and the life seems extraordinary, interesting, unique, full of surprises.

My conclusion: all of us have something to say. These essays are my reflection of that. They are my "shells" upon the sand and tides of one life.

Mine.

Amen

I say Amen as an ending, a completion. It is a good ending, a resolved one, but perhaps sometimes, an incomplete one — a relationship that has no way forward — so an Amen acknowledges that truth, for that moment.

The thing about Amen is that it does seem to end something — usually a prayer. We set an intention; we say some words; we say Amen. Then we leave, we eat, we go to sleep.

Every religion has this Ahhh sound, I have been told. Aum in the Buddhist tradition comes to mind; Allah as the name of God for the Muslims. In every case, it serves as a most holy word.

Then there are the humorous thoughts: Ah …. MEN! A group of women sighing over the idiosyncracies of men. Or AH, Men! A group of men happily together saying, oh boy, just us guys. Yeah.

From a sound perspective, I prefer Aum. The Mmmm seems to leave a door open, as though a transition is occurring rather than has occurred.

The Nnnn in Amen feels more like a door has closed — as though we have moved from sacred time to ordinary time.

In my spiritual life, the Amen moves me from sacred to ordinary, as though the two need to be divided in time. Now I'm "sacred", now I'm doing household chores, or arguing with my neighbor, or playing games on my iPad. No thought of sacred, no Amens.

Is there a way of carrying amen into *that* part of my life? Is there a way of being sacred in the ordinary? The Buddhists recommend that we stay in the present, that only the present can be holy.

If we said, A-main, as in re-main, perhaps that would remind us that Amen is not closure. Maybe we should end prayers with Remain. Remain in the Spirit; remain in hope; remain in faith; remain in the daily breath of present-moment. Remain.

I wonder what holds us back, and this draws me into studying the history of words, as used in culture, history, assumption. Does Amen hold us back or carry us forward?

If it weren't for that Nnnn. The Aaaa opens. Our mouth opens; our heart seems to vibrate, breath flows out. The Nnnn closes with a flick of the tongue that seals in the breath, trapping it within us. SURELY this must affect our bodily response to the divine. Open. Close. Open. Close. Then perhaps we are *sealing* the Spirit of the prayer within us, enclosing it in our body.

Admittedly, only a writer would wonder about such things. But the spiritual journey consists of such tiny moment-like times. When did God, a word, become man. Well, that's a big one; Amen is a little apostrophe on the heart of faith. Still, God-energy probably has no Amen at all. How could there be an Amen to creation, to love, to spirit?

In that sense, we live in an Amen-less world. Perhaps we should end each prayer with a breath—just to make sure we leave the door open for Spirit to flow in and out of us on the next breath, the next thought, the next action.

Ahhhh…..

Blessing

One could dissect this word into "Be less'ing — in other words, there might be a blessing in having "lessing" or less of something. We, in America, say we are blessed, and we are. We have two oceans that once could protect us from war. We have soil rich enough to sustain food for ourselves and much of the world. We have enough freedom to create, innovate, and invent.

Unfortunately, we often don't consider this a blessing. Rather, we believe we earned it. We aren't exactly grateful but rather proud of ourselves. So the blessing simply becomes an archaic word used on Sundays, because we are supposed to be grateful.

I remember visiting El Salvador during their civil war. I wanted to spend a day with a mother because I could only understand war through a mother's eyes.

I was a mother. I knew what it meant to be a mother. But I didn't know how you could nurture and care for a child in war.

I spent the day with Maria. I met her in the morning as she was hoisting a large tin wash basin filled with boiling water and field corn onto her head. We walked to a common spout pouring out water for a whole community.

She stepped into the water in her dress, stood beneath the spout to get cooling water, then began to scrub the kernels to free them from the starch.

Again and again, she returned to the pouring water until satisfied. Meanwhile her five-year-old daughter picked up kernels that splashed out of the tin. Not a single grain was lost.

Next she walked to a dark shed sheltering an ancient grinding machine operated by huge floor-to-ceiling belts. She poured the drained corn into the machine careful not to catch her hand. Out came corn meal ready for tortillas.

Finally we returned to her tin-roofed open air stall. Within was a sheet of metal, heated by rubbish-found cardboard.

She and her two older daughters began to rapidly make tortillas. No salt. No oil. No flavoring. Just cornmeal patted into thin cakes and cooked on metal.

Then she sold them for 3 cents each.

I thought her work day over, she could socialize, do her laundry, rest—it didn't seem such a bad life. One hour passed.

Vamanos!

I looked up from playing with her youngest daughter. Maria had another caldron of boiling corn on her head.

At that moment, I realized I would *always* know where Maria was; and she would never know where I was. My children might be taking piano lessons, playing at the park, on vacation, going to school. But I would see Maria, in my mind's eye, washing, grinding, cooking, selling in a hot tin shed.

When it was time to leave, I wanted to give Maria a gift. I had been told that Trail Mix, unattainable in El Salvador and certainly for Maria, would be a beautiful thank you gift. So I gave her the bag I had brought from America.

She opened it up, took a few pieces, gave a few pieces to each of her seven children. Then she walked through the entire village giving every one a portion of the Trail Mix.

She blessed an entire village.

Blessing. Be-less'ing. Be-Less ...

Compassion

"With passion" immediately comes to mind. To join with another in a passionate caring way. To *see* the other, try to walk in their shoes. Such thoughts immediately come to mind.

But then I think of my parents. Finnish descendents. Now, Finns are not warm-hearted pasta-loving Italians. I can see a compassionate Italian, hugging and kissing, offering red wine to resolve every human crisis—but being the child of two *Finnish* heritage parents does not evoke memories of passion, let alone *com*passion.

I remember my sister's woebegone words to me one day: "Dad never held me after I was two years old." Neither of us recall being held on a lap or swooped up for a hug or a kiss. We grew up like two icebergs, in a happy sense of that word.

I once espoused my sister's grievous childhood to my mother's sister, "We were NEVER hugged!" Aunt Alice looked at me disgustedly and said, "Finns don't hug." Somehow I found this wildly funny, and one childhood trauma got wiped off the charts.

So I have to scratch the surface deeper to find compassion, Finnish style. Surely it exists in every tradition—from Maui to Sierra Leone to Cuba, Libya, and Germany.

For the silent Finns, it's not the verbalized thought that counts but the *expression* of it.

I remember the day my husband suffered a heart crisis. Barely alive, code blue three times during the night, the doctors found the situation baffling. They withdrew treatments that were aggravating his condition, just giving him basic care.

Mom called me from Florida. "We'll be in Maryland in three days," she said and hung up.

Compassion. Finnish style.

My husband slowly recovered. With no departing hugs or kisses, Mom and Dad packed up their RV and drove away.

Today I have many friends who are compassion-masters. They lovingly hold my wounds, sometimes with laughter, sometimes with wine, sometimes with words or even silence.

The point is this: I *feel* heard and for me, that is compassion.

Then again, some of us are wired differently. Consider people who are born with Aspergers. It is possible that in their world, in their way, they may have more compassion.

They know what it is to be blocked emotionally—and that very knowing is the root of compassion.

Those of us who are born with no emotional handicap can find a multitude of ways to express our caring, whether a la Finnish or Hispanic.

I would like to believe that those who struggle on a daily basis with emotional expression in some way live out a deeper compassion, beyond words.

I sometimes feel a kinship with those diagnosed with Aspergers as I often need time alone to feel my feelings. I feel a bit awkward, a bit shy, a bit slow, a bit *Finnish*. However, the depth of my caring never feels uncertain or marginalized to me. If anything, when I am alone and quiet, I can feel heartfelt compassion flowing through me.

With passion.

Death

Neither my mother nor my sister wanted to be in the hospital room with my father as the nurse disconnected the life support. It was too wrenching. Nor did the floor nurses want family members in the room. I, on the other hand, didn't want Dad to die alone. Convincing the nurse I would not go hysterical, I witnessed this moment of passage.

It remains as vivid today as on April 15, 1987. The various machines beeped or showed green spikes on a monitor. Quietly the nurse turned off the life supports, one after another, telling me what each had supplied. Heart. Air. Nutrients. We watched as his heartbeat slowed, the peaks growing lower and slower.

I held his warm right hand, the nurse held his left. We waited. We watched. Then at some moment, I felt the room fill with light. There was a pause. Then he was gone.

Light. The room filled with light. What a strange thing to feel … not see. Later, I tried to find words. *It was as though a trapdoor in the cosmos opened. A shaft of light came into the room to gather Dad up. He looked back once with a huge smile. Then the trapdoor snapped shut, cutting me off from him forever.*

And I was PISSED.

He got to go; I was stuck on earth probably for a few more decades…

I realize most people don't want to die. I certainly don't. But Dad's death opened a chapter in my life. I found I could not grieve because that particular felt-sense of Light embodied an almost transcendent joy.

Thirteen years later, my mother neared the end of her life, consumed by Alzheimer's. She resided in a group home 3,000 miles away from me, with my sister being the major caretaker at the time. I went to see her. Mostly she sat in a chair with a clouded gaze. I cried with joy when I saw her; I cried when it came time to leave.

As I kneeled before her, she gripped my arms with her aged, bony hands, and looked directly into my eyes. What I saw was clearly not lights out, but lights elsewhere. I felt as though I was looking *through* her into *Spirit* directly, without human intervention. They were no longer human eyes nor diseased eyes, but eyes seeing into the *other* side. She was giving me a glimpse of what she was now seeing. There was a Divine *Bigness* to it.

Six weeks later, she was dead.

I find hope in these memories. Death doesn't quite live in time and space; it resides in *Light* and *Transcendency*. People who have near death experiences bring back radiant stories.

We live in other dimensions besides time. I experienced *Light* with my father, *Transcendence* with my mother.

Death, in a way, became birth—a birth as transcendent and light-filled as a newborn child entering our midst. Life. Death. Perhaps the distance between the two is no distance at all but the most radiant moment of *being*.

Eclipse

For weeks, I anxiously worried about the weather for our upcoming national solar eclipse. The Midwest has quirky summer weather. Flash thunderstorms. Drought. Dry lightning and thunder.

Sunday was beautiful. Monday, not. All of Missouri woke to that uncertain forecast which ranged from "cloudy", to "mostly cloudy", to "afternoon thunderstorms". I went onto my deck and balefully gazed at fat rolls of dark clouds interspersed with blue sky and fluffier clouds.

My river town hovered just outside the edge of the 70-mile swath of the total eclipse sweeping across the nation from Oregon to South Carolina. I could experience 99 percent of it. But …

I read the morning newspaper: "99 percent is like driving 99 out of a 100 miles to your favorite restaurant." "Ninety-nine is okay; but a hundred is a million times better."

I headed for the 100 percent, picking up my friend Toto on the way. We sped down empty country roads as the eclipse drew nearer and nearer to totality. We drove through hard rain, eyeballing where the dark behemoth of water might lighten to sullen gray.

We chose an unknown dead end road with fifteen minutes left. We sat in fold-out chairs in the middle of the street. Waiting.

The cicadas began to roar. The western sky precipitously darkened. In that eerie night, lightning flashed in the distance. Suddenly a cloud hole appeared and we *saw* the eclipse. At least 30 percent. The temperature dropped. A cool breeze stirred.

We sat in the middle of a total solar eclipse we could not see.

The sun, gauzy behind thin clouds, showed once again, this time 90 percent as the moon began to separate from its co-joined moment with the sun. Minutes later, the day — as we know it — returned.

I wanted to think big thoughts, have big feelings. I wanted to be transported to some eclipse-type ecstasy.

I also wanted to let go of having to have an "experience."

As I ping-ponged between letting go and grasping, I *did* realize that the cosmic alignment of earth, moon, and sun *would* occur without my input. I like to think some beautiful energy of love flowed between these three beautiful galactic creations. Even more hopeful, I wanted to just *stand* within a total eclipse.

Seeing it became less important than experiencing the journey into dark, then light.

I could have sat on my deck. The view, I am told, was better. Cloudy but more transparent. But I loved driving down unknown two-lane back roads at breakneck speeds, seeking totality. Sitting on a lawn chair in the middle of a dead-end road. Looking to the west where dark clouds and thunder met unnatural night. Listening to thousands of cicadas screeching in cacophony. I breathed *in* the totality of the eclipse—and *out*.

In a way, I loved *not* seeing it. Why? Because sometimes being blind is the best way to see. If I had *seen* the full eclipse, I would have told myself I captured it. Owned it. I won over the weather. I added totality to my collection of prized moments.

Instead, the eclipse captured *me*. I simply sat. In a totality I could not see or own.

I was *totally* there.

Forgiveness

It's hard to look at this from a lofty perch right now, as I have recently experienced feeling hurt. The emotional pain seems to ricochet, hitting one of us, then the other. Yet a strange "knowing" immediately affected me. I realized, even at the height of my pain: *I love you*. And ironically, here I am—having landed on the letter F. Forgiveness.

I remember decades ago, I also felt wounded in a relationship. I sat in a darkened chapel, remembering a gospel passage that what is bound on earth is bound in heaven.

What if this person died today? Tomorrow? I wondered. *I wouldn't want this person carrying my refusal to forgive into the afterlife.* But I wasn't ready to forgive. I was angry.

So I made a commitment. I "fore-gave" this person right then, completely and absolutely. I realized it might take a lifetime to forgive them in my heart, but I wanted them to go free right then.

I realized that my fore-giveness was more a commitment than a reality. Today, 25 years later, I can't even remember the person—or the event.

Today, I feel hurt *and* I feel love. I don't know where forgiveness is in such a situation.

First, even the word seems problematic. For *me* to forgive anyone else implies that I believe I stand in a superior position—somehow having the power to *bequeath* forgiveness.

Other words seem more heart-felt. *Accepting* what has transpired comes to mind. It happened. It hurt. It changes things. We can't go back. We may not recover. And … it's okay. It has absolutely nothing to do with love.

Love exists when real-life relationships may not. Strange as it may seem, I can love this person—and know it serves neither of us to attempt to fix, ignore, or bury this moment.

If I see no way forward, that does not mean we both will not go forward.

Forgiveness means we have to take ourselves into account. I think it wiser to forgive myself, honor myself, respect myself—and acknowledge the breakage at its deepest levels.

This is painful. It evokes fear, sadness, grief, a sense of profound loss, a desperate desire to fix things, to walk it back, to get back to where we were. All of that needs heartfelt forgiveness.

Acknowledging the other person's reality and deeply accepting it as very real for them, and true for them, and unalterable for them, also has the kernels of forgiveness.

Sometimes the heart, strangely, sees more clearly than the mind or the emotions.

find myself surprised that my love for this person sails along, peacefully; my mind and emotions still roiling.

Hard as it seems, I believe the heart knows the best way forward. Forgiveness is a force of life. When it is loveless, it is the ego benevolently granting a gift to a "lesser" person. But with love, no forgiveness is really necessary. What could there be to forgive?

Grace

Grace intersects with our human world in much the way Spirit does—lightly, invisibly, but with profound effect. I might have attempted describing my sense of grace rather mentally, if grace didn't actually hit me over the head … today.

Let me start this story about a year ago. Sometimes we have friendships that reside strong and deep within us. Time can pass; distance can occur; but that heart-sense of oneness persists. Angelita , Corinna, and I have enjoyed that type of soul-level love. Yet we are all single women living independent lives. Our relatives don't necessarily know we exist. And if one of us dies … who knows to tell us?

Angelita died about a year ago, after suffering for decades from an untreatable condition. Corinna learned from a friend that Angelita had passed over, but had no details. She called me but no Google or Facebook information appeared, no obituary, no funeral home. And Angelita's name was actually Bonnie.

Angelita had a sister, but we didn't know her name. So we grieved; we knew Angelita was gone from our lives; but we felt a piece was missing.

Passings are important. They are births into spirit — and we missed the awesome moment. We didn't even know it had happened till weeks later.

So yesterday I clicked *Messenger* on my iPhone. I glanced (as I recall) at those active at the moment. I noticed that "Many Hands" — the leader of the Native American community Angelita belonged to — was on. We have never friended each other; I've never met him; he doesn't know I even exist. Yet here he was — "online." Shocked, I quickly messaged him asking for information about Angelita. The day passed with no response.

Then today, Sunday, I received a message from a woman I didn't know. It read, "I'm sister to Angelita Rae and I need to talk to you about her so please call me back."

Immediately, I clicked on her number. A voice very much like Angelita's — deep with a bit of rough — answered, and an astonishing conversation began.

"She died one year ago today," a woman who pronounced her name Ma-rye-a, told me. "In the end they couldn't stop the bleeding. They tried several times and finally the doctors said there was nothing else they could do. Seven days later, she died."

Although she left not a single word about end-of-life wishes, she was very clear about how her body was to be handled.

In Native American tradition, she was to be washed by her sister and two dear friends, her waist-long silver hair combed in a specific way. She chose the dress to be buried in, wrapped in the sacred shawl I had woven her years ago, and then placed in a particular blanket.

With her drum, her pipe, and her eagle feather, as she requested, she was laid to rest.

"We could not find a telephone list anywhere; we had no way to contact you or Corinna," Ma-rye-a lamented.

She went on, "Angelita wanted us to celebrate her life on this first anniversary with a sacred give-away in the Native American tradition. Many Hands has received Angelita's sacred objects for the give-away."

She added that she would give other items of Angelita's away to friends tonight. They would celebrate her life with drumming, song, and sharing.

Ma-rye-a told me, "I realized as I touched her things that everything was sacred. She saw such beauty in each item in her dwelling.

As we hung up, I promised to join them that evening. I created an altar with the drum she had made me so many years ago, the shawl she had blessed at my naming ceremony, a carved tortoise made of properly harvested woolly mammoth tusks, and a candle which burned all day.

Grace always unexpected, is a blessing. How in the world could Many Hands have appeared on my phone, allowing me to find Angelita's sister—one day before the anniversary of her death?

This, for me, is amazing *Grace*.

Humility

I am not sure that we, as Americans, have much of an understanding of humility. America seems built on pride. We honor our independent nature; we say we are a can-do nation. We consider ourselves a super power—the strongest nation in the world.

We have little experience of being humbled, and when we are, it is in the wrong sense of the word.

We felt humbled by our lack of victory in Vietnam. We felt humiliated by 9-11. We feel no pride in our continuing military presence in Afghanistan. We feel shame when terrorism strikes on our own cities and streets.

But that humility has its roots in national patriotic ego. Like the Hatfields and McCoys, winning, losing, winning, losing, pride, humiliation, pride, humiliation—it all has a certain ego-stuckness to it.

I look at my own life and can certainly find numerous moments of ego stuckness, and I see a huge difference between humiliation and humility.

We immediately recognize moments of humility in our midst when we see it.

Nelson Mandela, after years in prison, witnessed to the humanity in his guards. The Dalai Lama deepened his love for all people after losing his own holy land, Tibet.

Desmond Tutu learned to look beyond racism. Mother Teresa served the most destitute; Abraham Lincoln saw all of us within one nation. Martin Luther King recognized death might be the inevitable answer to his hunger for inclusiveness.

Humbleness seems to grow only in good soil — the daily tilled soil of a soul absolutely committed to love for others, regardless of the circumstances. It seems to reach a critical mass when the self sees itself as a servant to the larger Self.

A good friend of mine always prays the same way: for the best possible outcome. Whatever the situation — disease, war, ruptured relationship — she asks for the best possible outcome for all parties. She doesn't presume to *know* what that outcome might be. At that moment, she unites herself with *humility*. She becomes humble.

I think we need to pay attention to all our moments of humility. They are there, buried beneath our very practical ego-centered moments.

There are times when we impulsively respond towards the good in others.

We put others first — not because we've decided, mentally, it is the right thing to do. Rather, the heart races forward, ahead of the mind, and just does the right thing for that moment. Perhaps very out of character. Perhaps a great surprise to oneself. Nevertheless, the moment, the action, the thought, tills the soil of the soul. Because the ego has not the time to think about what it wants, the moment itself bonds with humility. It allows humility to fertilize the world with an unmistakable goodness, a love, a movement forward and uplifting, for all of humanity.

Unfortunately, after the moment, the ego often races in to take pride of ownership. Humility slips into the shadows. But we must never forget that *in the moment* a certain humility-of-action-and-caring stepped forward, front stage, and *acted*.

We need to remember those moments. Cherish them. Nurture and encourage them. And know, with gratitude, that we embodied, for a moment, the beautiful human quality of heart ... humility.

Indwelling

To me, indwelling means to go within, to abide within, to stay put — for a while — within oneself. Often an uncomfortable task. We get itchy sitting still, nervous about looking within, let alone *sitting* with it.

But there is another kind of indwelling: relaxing on your favorite sofa with a cup of tea; staring mindlessly out your window; unwinding in front of the TV.

Indwelling means creating balance between your "outside" world of work and responsibilities, and your "inside" world of self care.

My daughter visited me recently, and politely made no comments about how I decorated my home. One room, once a rather boring wallpapered dining room, now looked as though it were a five-walled Impressionist painting. The only subdued color, from her perspective, was probably the dark sage rug.

Add to that round-the-room bookcases, filled, plus knickknacks atop them, and the overall effect either evoked awe and joy — or, in my daughter's case, the feeling she'd entered a color-saturated nightmare.

The other rooms, loaded with art, also failed the zen test.

Now, my daughter's life and mine are quite different. As an architect, she multi-tasks between renovations, additions, and new buildings like a ping pong ball. Add to that the generally congestive East Coast life and marriage, her everyday life is bombarded by tasks, people, and sensory overload. The last thing she'd want to come home to would be a color-overloaded house. She prefers cool grays, quieting whites, and simple lines.

I, on the other hand, live alone. Hours quietly go by. I weave. I write. As an older woman, I move a bit slower through house cleaning, bills, and cooking. I *am* zen.

In other words, we both are creating very necessary balance. She goes for muted tones. I go for stimulation.

So to properly indwell, we must take into account our personal circumstances. Our home needs to balance our out-dwelling world. We certainly don't want more of the same. I no more need a quiet outer world without friends, than my daughter needs to come home to a cluttered, color-filled extravaganza.

Of course, there exists a deeper sense of indwelling where a sense of peace, connectedness, safety, and relaxation supports us.

That is a kind of holy indwelling, an invitation to Spirit.

Surprisingly, it is probably easier for me to enter that inner space, despite my color-filled house, because I live alone, in silence. Nevertheless, I have to sit. Still. Silent. Emptying mental chatter. Deep indwelling, like water drawn from a well, requires the bucket to go down.

My daughter is still young, and busy. But she has begun her indwelling by creating balance. She indwells when she sinks into her gray-upholstered sofa. She silently watches a bit of TV. She unwinds. Even if there is sound from the TV, or conversations with her husband, she is indwelling — recovering from the multitasking, high paced, outer world. She is zen. In her home — a home designed to be still, quiet, peaceful.

We create the balance we need. Out-dwelling. Indwelling.

Joy

I mentally "toggled" between writing about joy … or justice. Actually, justice came to mind first, which perhaps says a great deal about our current societal interest in right and wrong these days. Our TV guides give us daily options from NCIS to Survival to SWAT teams, murder and mayhem. *So where's the joy*, I wonder, when even I get caught in the TV drama?

Joy is almost equivalent to *Grace*. It is an interior state, quite steady even in stormy waters. It has a bubbling quality like a hidden spring burbling its waters endlessly out, whether noticed or not. We all experience moments of joy: from holding a newborn to experiencing a stunning sunset or smelling the first hyacinth of spring. Such moments have a wordless quality.

Happiness is a more exterior state, momentary, based on circumstance. If I am very hungry and have the good fortune to indulge in a good meal, trust me—I'm happy. I feel sated; I am grateful; I feel at one with the world. Most importantly, I want to *talk* about it. I have an avalanche of words to describe this culinary experience. One would say, "Well, isn't that *joy*?

Perhaps the two—happiness and joy—co-join for a moment. But not necessarily.

Looking back, I suspect that my sense of *joy* comes from years of meditation (by the way, often sporadic with extended periods of drought ... meaning I don't meditate at all.)

Somewhere, somehow, in a bodily way I felt joy. I remember the story of Saint Bernadette — a less likely saint than one could imagine.

An illiterate village girl in France, who adhered to the daily practice of saying the rosary with as much fervor as any young child, fell one day into a mystical trance where she encountered — in a bodily way — the Virgin Mary.

She saw her, and talked to her.

After several meetings, Mary asked her to dig in a particular area and drink the water. Bernadette — in this mystical awareness — began to claw the dirt. At best, she unearthed muddy water, which she tried to drink.

Her village followers (who hoped that she was one of the blessed ones, a saint-to-be) were horrified and fled. She, upon coming to her senses, could make no more sense of it than they.

But the next day, a villager happened to pass by this same area, and clear spring water was flowing from this muddy scratched-out source. It became a stream of healing for many people and to this day is venerated.

Joy, I think, is like that. We dig into our psychic rubble through prayer—meditative, intentional, recited, weary—petitioning a connection with God. We dig where we have been told by religious history to dig. Often, for people with near death experiences, the waters of *joy* burst from within like an eruption. However it happens, once unearthed (surely by grace alone), the hidden spring of *Joy* surges out upon the earth of our life, irrepressible, entirely impossible to bury. It just *is*.

Happiness has no such equivalency. It appears like weather—a sunny, delightful, spring-like day with daffodils and tulips and intoxicating scents. Then it rains. Dark, sullen, stormy clouds. We are happy … we are unhappy (or sad or mad or frustrated or indifferent).

However, in those moments of happiness, there appears to be a wide, unencumbered connection to *joy* if we take the time to be aware. I eat the beautiful meal; I am ecstatically happy with my feeling of well-being; I pause to *feel* gratitude; in that moment, I am joined to *joy*. The two, happiness and joy, unite for a moment and flow together. The joy remains; the happiness fades.

Very strangely, joy abides even in the most discouraging moments. I have been depressed …and joy-filled; angry … and joyful; burdened with low self-esteem … and yet feel joy.

This is not spontaneous. I am not driving my car, feeling sad, and am suddenly overwhelmed by joy. Rather, I am sitting with my sadness in a deliberate thoughtful way; I enter into silence; and I find *joy* waiting to greet me, still there — flowing steadily through my being.

There is an irony here. Two seemingly opposing emotions should not co-exist. But *joy* comes from a different source than happiness or sadness; it comes from Grace, Divine Love, Spirit. It is unencumbered by the emotional weather patterns we experience as humans.

Joy just *is*. It provides the ballast to our lives. When I re-engage in my daily tasks, I may still feel sad or angry or depressed. *Joy* does not seem to solve my dilemmas; rather, it tells me, *I am here*. It is the contrast of opposites. Because of *joy*, I can see the humor in my human dilemma; I *see* what I am doing to myself. I am wallowing in my self-imposed suffering. *Joy*, like a mother, stays by my side until the emotional weather storm I am experiencing has passed.

And I know, with gratitude, that *joy* will be there when the next storm hits.

Kinship

When I think of kinship, tribal ties comes to mind. I am born to a certain family in a certain place in a certain socioeconomic status — that is my tribe.

Presumably that is where I'll feel safest, and most at home. I'm born there; I'll die there. I know without having to explain the values, laws, subtle signs of my group.

We have multiple kinships. Kinship to family; kinship to our generation; kinship to the vocation we choose, kinship to the religion or spirituality we follow. Each clusters around an entirely different set of people.

I remember stumbling across this seemingly obvious fact when I realized my mother was a *person*, a real human being with her own friends, her own story.

Of course I didn't understand this until she was knee-deep into memory loss.

That's when I started talking about her with her lifelong friends Mim, Beulah, Jane, and sister Alice. The wake-up moment came when Mim told me this story …

"When your mother was newly married, she and Herby had an icebox for their refrigerator.

It had a motor on top that vibrated so much the fridge would walk across the kitchen floor every day. Your mother would complain and Herby would push it back into the corner instead of fixing the problem.

Finally, one day Elsie got so mad she painted the refrigerator PURPLE. That was the one color your dad hated. She figured maybe he'd *see* it if it was painted purple, and finally fix it."

By this time, I was laughing almost to fall off my chair. I remembered that icebox. It ended up in our basement as a backup fridge—and it was paint-brushed white.

I always wondered why anyone would paint a white refrigerator white.

Mim ended the story, "Oh, it got fixed. But she never said a word, and he never said a word."

THAT, I knew well enough, was from our Finnish tradition—our tribe. Finns don't rant and rave. A purple refrigerator would be the perfect expression of a Finnish argument.

Needless to say, I have inherited this trait (though not nearly as creatively). It comes from my familial kinship.

But that day, I realized that Mom and her friends, all of whom had men who fought in World War II, had a language all their own, a silent language which only they could understand.

It didn't need nuancing or even telling. But we, the sons and daughters, didn't know or speak this language. It belonged to their tribe, not ours.

My daughters will not understand my lived kinship through the turbulent 60s and 70s, nor will I understand theirs.

Rarely do all our kinship needs get met within the family.

Artists and accountants, physicists and mystics, football players and piano teachers would seem to have little kinship. Courtesy, of course. Respect, yes. But soul-understanding, encouragement, nurturing, deep friendship would be a certain leap-of-kinship.

Love itself most likely provides the best glue to cross natural kinship lines. Witness Romeo and Juliet. They leapt impulsively across kinship boundaries only to be crushed by them.

Today, we have strongly entrenched political, geopolitical, religious, and economic kinships with moats and drawbridges.

We are in the thrall of a certain kind of kinship.

Astronaut Scott Kelly, who spent a year in space, commented that he could not see any national boundaries on Earth. He saw no tribal kinships from his Space Station.

Kinship can be viewed from the me-perspective.

Such kinship goes like this: Me. My family. My community. My country. My Earth. Or: Me. My friends. My likes and dislikes. My belief system. My life. My Earth.

Unfortunately, these kinship systems, by implication, need an other — one who is *not* me.

It's becoming clear that this kinship system is most likely doomed to extinction.

With over seven billion human beings on one planet, all focused on me (personally, politically, environmentally, geographically), self survival on spaceship Earth in the kinship mode is increasingly, directly opposed to survival.

Consider that the goal of every kinship model is to feel safe and loved.

To accomplish, this we've created so many protective structures, from religion to defense, that we are literally being crushed to death beneath the weight (and cost) of them.

When every kinship system seems to be cracking under the sheer weight of its me-ness, the best place to start the transformation out of me-ness to One-ness is within the "me".

I recently read a Facebook entry where one woman—not knowing how to solve all the problems of the world said that she decided to work on her own battlefield, fighting her own wars to clear out obsolete kinship systems that harmed others and the planet Earth.

Her model is simple. Her tools: love, respect, self-reflection, good action.

It can transform families, communities, countries, planets, friendships, vocations, and actions.

That seems to be a big enough battlefield for any one of us.

Levity

Nothing seems to be in shorter supply in our modern stressed society than levity. We have become terribly serious, and with good reason. We receive 24-hour news about climate, differing religions, politics, socioeconomic divides, terrorism, starvation, etc. Under such circumstances, it seems sacrilegious to say there is a serious world-wide shortage of levity.

Yet ... there is.

Levity swings the pendulum from one extreme to the other, with the intention of allowing the pendulum to come to rest at the center. It looks at the world with a skewed lever of logic, using laughter as its source of equanimity, balance, hope, and optimism. Quite different than cracking a good joke (though an added bonus), some people seem endowed with intellectual gravitas for levity. The "levites" have happy wrinkles around their mouth and their eyes seem to dance with a kind of inner bubbling humor. They seem to see a different world than many of us.

What exactly is levity? The Webster's *Dictionary* condemns it as "a disrespectful way of considering serious things." That sounds a bit outdated to me.

American culture of the 50's predated Vietnam, birth control, the women's movement, drug epidemics, and Watergate. We lived in a black-and-white TV world of *I Love Lucy*, *Leave it to Beaver*, and *The Andy Griffith Show*.

Our world today seems out-of-control. We are *expressing* ourselves verbally and physically. The overall felt sense is one of chaos, disorder, and destruction.

Levity levels the psychic field. It provides much needed balance. It is, in fact, disrespectful of serious things—necessarily so.

What needs leavening today? Who needs "levitating"?

Obviously ... the *other*. The one who has the exact opposite (read, *wrong*) viewpoint. *Saturday Night Live*, *The Kimmel Show*, John Stewart ... we laugh uproariously at their *stupidity* (and they laugh at ours). This meets the classic *Webster's Dictionary* definition.

The best levity, however, punctures our own balloons rather than others. We are best served, not by inflicting levity upon our enemies, but upon our own mindsets which we absolutely believe should be the only truth.

Today it seems absolutely correct to make fun of anyone who fails to agree with us, but it perpetuates our bubble-world.

I would be far more benefited by puncturing my own balloon, hard though that may be.

So, for me, climate change is a big deal. I worry about polar bears, plastic in our blood stream, rivers, and oceans. I have suspicions about Monsanto's concern for planet Earth.

I see nothing to joke about. I am zero on the scale of levity. I prefer to rail against "the enemy" — whoever I decide, on that day, in that moment, it to be.

Is there *any* room for levity?

It reminds me of a day when my sister Sandra and her husband Ed and I were visiting my mother in Florida. When we walked in, we got the set of rules.

(1) Do NOT open the curtains. Too much sun, too hot, too much air conditioning.

(2) Put *every* bit of garbage into the plastic tubes that the newspaper comes in; knot it; and put it in the trash can. Possible cockroaches, ants, flies.

(3) Put *everything* back where it belongs. Misplaced means lost, after we leave.

We dutifully followed these *serious* rules every visit for years, until Mom could no longer remember, needed assisted care, and moved out of her home.

On *that* day, Ed *threw open* the curtains, urging the sun to come in and destroy the air conditioner. He heaved coffee grounds into the trash can, liberated from the plastic newspaper tube. We left a ton of stuff out on the kitchen counter.

And we laughed. Almost to the point of hysteria.

We were railing against loss, using levity as our weapon. Our mother could no longer be our mother. She would never come home to slam the curtains shut, proffer plastic bags, or scowl at us for leaving household items out.

True to *Webster's Dictionary*, our levity was disrespectful ... of aging. Of death. Of loss.

It provided balance, release, hope, and yes, love. If we hadn't loved our mother, there would have been no need for levity.

Levity provides the leavening needed to lift the heavy dough of life into something new. A new way of seeing, solving, moving forward.

Levity, properly used, is love.

Manageability

When I wake up, I lay in bed to plan my day — to make it manageable. It all sounds very nice, in bed, when I am resting in a totally prone position with my head snuggled into my favorite pillow. The dog is snoring; the cat cordoned off in my office; the cockatiel perching in his cage in the still-dark living room.

Then I get up, and right away my managed day starts to fray. First I let Pumpkin-the-cat out of the office. He stretches, stops by the scratching post, jumps into the sink. My job is to rub his chin and turn on the faucet, leaving him to slurp up running water. Next stop, the dog crate. Brianna, my corgi, bolts out, racing to the office in hopes of finding cat throw up. Getting no reward from her morning hunt, she awaits breakfast, standing on her hind feet, whining.

I let the dog outdoors for her morning duties, along with the cat. I then quarantine both so I can take the cockatiel Him-Laya out of his cage — safely assuming the dog and cat will not eat him. He sits on my finger as we go to the bathroom and close the door. I fill a syringe with his medicine, wait for him to stop flying, throw a towel over him, unearth his neck, and shoot the meds into his opened mouth.

THAT is my "managed" morning—and I haven't even had my cup of *very strong* tea.

Somehow this totally *managed* morning can quickly veer into unmanaged: the cat *has* thrown up; the dog *doesn't* poop; the bird *spits out* his medicine.

Then, the very start of my day teeters into unmanaged. (None of this compares to parenting school-age children who open the day with the thrill of unmanageability.)

I no longer measure manageability by what I think I ought to get done in a day. I can lay in bed full of my optimistic "oughts", but place no expectations upon them.

This extends far beyond my day. It redirects my life.

For example, house size. About twenty years ago I decided that the proper size of a house was one in which I used every room every day.

That comes to about 1200 square feet for me, with a large chunk going to the weaving/writing room. I can foresee dropping about 400 square feet in the next ten years. I'm starting to look at downsizing.

Do I want to "manage" vacuuming when sweeping is easier and quieter? Is it time to find new homes for books, art, some furniture?

To me, manageable means I can flow through my day with reasonable civility.

If I find myself exhausted, stressed, crashing into bed like an overworked victim of my own making, I've become unmanaged (unhinged might be a better word).

I've slowly watched my yard-become-garden become garden-being-unmanageable. When I moved here, right by the Mississippi River, with stairs from town leading up to our Hannibal lighthouse, I wanted folks to see something pretty as they mounted the 250+ steps — especially on a hot humid Missouri day. So I started planting things: shrubs, pathways, patios, rose bushes, uncountable bulbs. I even dragged my enamel tub into a quaint setting.

Everything looked fresh and young and beautiful — and totally manageable. Over the years, the whole yard became a garden. I left one cosmetic patch of grass that I hand mow in about five minutes. My greatest challenge was the cliff: a periwinkle-and-wild-rose perilous hill abutting one side of my property. I clung to roots as I swung from bottom to top, side to side, clipping runaway saplings, tenacious vines, and unwanted weeds.

In my early 60s, I felt heroic: a garden mountain climber. At 70 not so much. I hired Shang.

Yesterday morning, as I lay in bed, I admitted, *I can't do this much anymore. It's totally unmanageable.* I see moving one day, but not yet. This is my beloved patch of yard-on-earth.

I felt a totally new thought float into my head. *Change the word from garden to habitat. All your exhaustion is coming from trying to make your yard beautiful. What if you created a beautiful habitat for the birds, butterflies, ground creatures?*

I pondered that with some excitement. The yard may end up looking unkempt. I can see milkweed, serviceberry and butterfly bushes running rampant—untrimmed.

It sounds … manageable.

Naming

We name too many things. In fact, we don't feel at all comfortable unless we *have* a name for something. Even a walk in the woods can raise a cacophony of questions: what is the name of that plant, that tree? Of course we overlook the familiar, hardly seeing it—but an unexpected blossom, an interesting leaf, and I, at least, want a *name*.

The same could go for a car I've never seen, a new vegetable in the grocery store, a person I haven't met.

It's like we're at this continuous never-ending cocktail party: "What do you do? Where do you work? Are you married? How many children do you have?" If we can name ourselves, to self and others, then there is a certain sense of safety. *Everything is okay here.*

I love names. Being raised by a father who admired Einstein over God (he was a nonbeliever), science is *loaded* with names. Identifying the unidentifiable—the quest for knowledge—seems unquenchable.

So when I meet someone who wants to just *be* with a tree or a plant or an animal, it seems almost unfathomable.

A few years ago, I became inexplicably drawn to experience "nature communication."

I honestly cannot remember how or why, and also honestly, I felt I had absolutely no credentials to communicate with any non-human being. Heck, I had enough trouble communicating with my family and friends.

Given my hesitation, and a deep sense of inadequacy, I began to participate in a teleconferencing experience with a skilled nature communicator. Within fifteen minutes of our first session, she said, "Okay, let's take some time to be with *Mystery Being #1*.

WHAT?! I thought to myself. Nevertheless we quieted down to be with ... nothing (in my mind). But hesitantly, I sensed a kind of bubbly bouncy happy energy. To my surprise, a woman in Oregon, and a man in Canada, another in Washington had similar experiences.

I know the reader immediately wants to know ... "Well, what was it? What was its *name*. If I don't offer that link, we feel "unlinked." (It was a grasshopper.)

Our teacher explains that our ability in this area is as natural as breathing; our culture has just strongly emphasized mind over relationship. Our biggest obstacle, it turns out, is doubt. And our doubt is rooted in our need to name things.

It's taken years for me to trust my relationship ability at least as much as my naming necessity.

We are much less able to name experiences of mystery, joy, love, transformation. There are times when events happen that are unnamable. Holding your newborn child for the first time — a miracle. A sunset, double rainbow, the red rocks of Sedona, Northern lights.

True, I am naming the event — but I cannot name the *effect* of the event.

We live in so much mystery. It is vast and wonderful. Yet we try to reduce it to a name. A thimble full of consciousness. We remove it from relationship to object, and in doing so, we feel in control, comfortable, in power *over* it.

Of course, the grasshopper could care less. It hops by, joyous, bouncy, and care free.

Out ...

When I decided to write these A-Z essays, I took a blank sheet of paper and as fast as I could, wrote down 26 words, "openness" grabbing the spot for O.

But this morning I found that I didn't *feel* like writing about openness. Maybe the word bores me, or I think too much has already been written about it.

For whatever reason, I opened up *Webster's Concise Desk Dictionary*. Heaven forbid, I would open the ten-pound ancient *Webster's International Dictionary* that molders under my desk, rarely used but much revered.

At any rate, I came to the word "out" and found myself absolutely fascinated by all the outs in our lives.

Here is a short list of *some* outs: outbid, outboard, outbreak, outcast, outclass, outcrop, outdated, outdoor, outfit, outgrow, outing, outlaw, outlay, outline, outlive, outmoded, outnumber, out-of-pocket, outpouring, outright, outset, outshine, outside, outsmart, outspoken, outstanding, out box, outward, outwit.

Imagine such a versatile word. It might very well be the most used word-in-combination of any in the English language. We can "out" anything—even ourselves.

I could *outline* an essay about an *outbreak* by *outcasts* who *outgrew* their confining *outdated outfits*, and decided they *outnumbered* their guards, and went *outdoors* and *outside* to *outshine* each other in their *outspokenness* of *outright* rage, hoping to *outwit* and *outsmart* their guards.

Put together like that, one clearly gets the sense that "out" has a wonderful freeing rebellious type quality.

It stands opposed to the norm, to the culture, to the status quo, to the same-as. We "outcast" ourselves in order to allow something new and different (and we hope better) to arise.

Society desperately needs these many avenues-of-out—from outcrops to outrage. It is our evolutionary edge, the way we can transform ourselves. In a way Charles Darwin, an outlier himself, described how all living beings, genetically change by this glacially slow evolution.

But each of us has "outs" within ourselves—places where we believe we don't fit.

My sister once told me, "I want everything that society wants of me. I want to be married and raise kids. The only thing I hate is the PTA."

Then she added, "You don't agree with anything. That's why life is so difficult for you."

I thought this very wise, hilariously funny, and very comforting. *Oh,* I said to myself, *I'm a zygot.* An environmental radicalist once called herself a zygot—the one in the family who doesn't fit. She is the woman who uses no toxins to clean, who saves used bath water to flush toilets (even though they live on well water), who buys and wears organic clothing, a die-hard "Granola Mom." Once we attempted to write a book together. I wanted to know what went on behind closed doors in the home of an environmental radicalist. I portrayed the toxin-using, bottle-toting, bleaching queen who peeled off tree-killing paper towels with savage glee. She had *no* paper towels in her house ... ever.

My zygotism seems much more tame in comparison. My parents and sister simply liked the societal status quo; I thought we deserved change. I was the outlier (much loved but not understood).

One day, I am told, my sister and mother were sitting at the breakfast table lamenting my strangeness. Now, we have one unknown branch of our family tree: my father's father. No one knows who he was. Sandra exclaimed, "She must have come from *his* side of the family." Mom, happy to have discovered my variant "root", bifurcated my birth into *that* branch of our genealogical tree, saying, "She sure isn't like us."

Once an outlier accepts their differentness, the whole world opens. If you're already weird, the out-words become friendly places to visit. I can be *outspoken* AND *outlandish*.

Like being a speck of salt in a pepper shaker, society's outliers do have a purpose. They shine a light on the future. It may not end up *being* the future. After all, it is just one possible future among many possibilities. But it has the *potential* for societal evolution to an even better, more equitable, peaceful, loving world.

How *outstanding*.

Potential

Potential has the same problem, or dilemma, as faith. It finds its potency in the unknown future.

Just as faith finds its greatest strength in *not* knowing, but trusting, potential poses the same type of no guarantees. "I shoot an arrow in the air, I know not where…"

Yet, potential applies much more to the human condition; faith, the divine.

We see potential in ourselves, our children, our friends. We are like rosebuds not yet opened.

The full and absolute potential of the rose is guaranteed, certified, by its genetic inheritance.

But wind, rain, frost, pestilence, heat, drought—a dozen things can rob the rosebud of its potential blossom and fragrance.

There's no point in asking the rose how it feels about this.

"Aren't you a bit disappointed in your performance? Here you are, planted in the Queen's royal garden, and you couldn't even produce one bloom."

This, of course, is how humans consider their potential. All too often we feel we missed the mark; we did too little.

I fondly remember a paragraph from one of the many books Thomas Merton, the famous American mystic, wrote. In it, he remembers consoling a man who had failed in every endeavor.

Merton said, "Well, your job is to fail."

I have looked high and low for that quote, but it certainly got stored in my unforgettable database. I think, at the time, I could relate very much to failing.

My job had ended, as had my marriage. My kids were teens—not conducive to feeling successful as a parent. The three pillars of success: career, marriage, parenting, all seemed in the trashcan.

Whatever potential I hoped for in myself, I had crash landed in the reality of my life.

I admire the people who tell me, "I knew from the time I was ten that I wanted to be a ... surgeon/lawyer/artist/writer/violinist. I, along with most of my friends, had no such certainty.

I lived in a vague sort of optimism.

I had potential and proceeded along that assumption. I got educated. I made reasonable grades. I got an interesting job.

But was this my potential? Meeting my potential? Most of us stumble into what we are good at, and build a life off of that (if we're lucky).

No matter my job, management would somehow end up at my desk asking me to write.

The first time occurred when I submitted my annual budget request for the library of a computer firm. In those days, if times were tight, the library was the first to go.

So I wrote vignettes about how our library had dramatically saved the day—finding past contract experience, pulling the right book for a scientist. I catalogued how many people stepped through our doors.

At any rate, the Vice President of whatever called me on the phone. "I couldn't stop reading your budget request." That really surprised me.

I got my budget—but was *this* my potential?

Maybe I am like a rose bush. I have loads of buds. Some open; some don't. Some years are good, some bad. The rose succeeds, fails. Sometimes, like Merton's man, it does nothing but fail.

But the rose bush could care less.

It doesn't equate success with potential. If it were to score itself, it'd probably say, "Oh, I have 100% potential all the time. Every year. Till I die. I don't control the weather, the soil, the water. Actually, if there's drought and I put out one blossom … I've met my 100% potential.

We are all born with 100% potential. Given perfect parenting, perfect environment, perfect opportunity — we'll *be* our potential.

But I think we're looking in the wrong direction. My potential is this: to be as deeply "me" on any given day. It may be me-as-grumpy, me-as-organized, me-as-failure, me-as-wildly successful. The only constant — just as for the rose bush — is to simply be … me.

That is my potential.

Quietness

Can there be quietness in the noise? Admittedly, we are a very noisy society. We lean toward valuing business sociability—chattiness by the workplace coffee pot, coworkers' birthdays, interminable meetings.

We drive with our radio on; we use uncountable household appliances that all make noise. Who remembers sweeping with a broom? Who washes dishes by hand?

We watch TV or Netflix or movies from Amazon Prime. Often we fall asleep listening to the soft background sounds of music, audible books, or TV. Our kids cannot do homework without sound.

I remember talking to one young woman who vividly remembered driving across the southwest desert with a broken radio. "I almost got hysterical," she admitted. The vast silence of the desert terrified her.

But given our everyday life, with all of its distractions, can we feel a sense of inner quietness? Personally, I think the answer is yes. But it is an acquired taste, often the offshoot of a meditative practice.

Meditation, when started, usually feels like a buzz saw—extraordinarily uncomfortable.

Our brains sizzle like hot eggs on a grill. Worse, the external noise around us seems amplified by our inner mind-chattering noise.

Over time, however, we do experience moments of quietness, and once we are reacquainted with this kind of stillness, we can expand these times from the meditation chair to the outdoors — the garden, walking the dog, fishing, stargazing.

I also think quietness can have an everyday "pacing" quality. Once I wondered how slow I'd have to walk to stay in touch with this inner world of silence, repose, peace.

I began walking down my gravel driveway at my normal pace. I didn't have a hint of silence. I began to slow my steps, slower and slower. In the end, I had to walk pretty slow to truly stay in touch with my inner quiet world.

During one five-year period of my life, I studied silence by living within its embrace. I created a silent, solitary lifestyle, without TV or radio or newspaper.

Notably, my connection to the calendar — to time itself — became erratic. I actually found that to be one of the strangest side effects of my personal experience with cultivated silence.

At any rate, during my initial forays into silence, I sometimes found myself on a subway going to D.C. With time on my hands, I would decide to meditate.

Eventually I learned to dive under the noise, like a swimmer going beneath the roar of a crashing surf. Everything around me became muffled.

So I suspect that we *can* experience quiet in a noisy environment.

Sometimes I join friends for a glass of wine in town. The acoustics are dreadful. If it happens to be crowded, there is an almost unbearable roar. You cannot really converse without raising your voice.

In those moments, I love to just go silent and listen to the roar. It has unbelievable vitality. I truly feel and enjoy my own quietness in those moments. I can't explain why.

I enjoy being with good dear friends. I haven't much to say. They continue to talk with enthusiasm and animation. I can join in; but it's also okay to savor an inner silence.

Our society truly needs to remember quietness. Without some inner silence, we lose our bearings.

These are the moments when we can't make decisions. We are like shuttle cocks being batted back and forth by our inner noise *and* the outer noise.

Often we try to drown the inner noise *with* outer noise because frankly, we are afraid of quietness.

If, however, we can befriend silence, sit in quietness, walk through our lives so that the inner and outer voices can talk to each other, then our inner sense of wisdom will reveal itself. Guidance will erupt. Good decisions are simply seen and made. Life flows.

Then we live in quietness … in our noisy world.

Rut

We know when we're in one. A rut. We might not admit it to anyone else, but secretly we see a sameness stretching into an endless future. I'm in a mini-rut right now. Not much inspires me, though I have to admit, walking my dog in our near-by park this morning, with the sugar maple leaves completely covering the walk, and the sun shining through the tree limbs felt like a non-rut moment.

Ruts, I've decided, have their usefulness. I remember the time our Trail Club at the University of Maryland decided we should try to walk 50 miles, nonstop, along the Towpath from Georgetown, Washington, D.C. to Harpers Ferry, West Virginia. It was during President Kennedy's advocacy of exercise.

In the end, our "group" consisted of five hikers which became three after about 20 miles. We started after our last classes, which put us on the trail around 5:00 PM on a nice spring evening. We planned to walk through the night.

Soon enough, we were walking in moonlit darkness. I walked right off the trail into the canal filled with water.

My boots and socks now soaking wet, I climbed out of the ditch wondering how I'd walk 50 miles without a flashlight.

We had decided when we left our cars that flashlights would slow us down.

That was when I noticed the *rut*. In fact, *two* ruts, made by years of foot traffic, mule-towing barge traffic, and bicycle traffic. I began to walk using my feet as sensors. It was easy enough to do. I felt absolute confidence that I'd not take another tumble into the canal as long as I stayed in my rut.

So ruts must have some beneficial purposes.

I often think back to our war on Iraq after 9/11. Our military moved so fast through the country as it headed for Baghdad.

I imagined myself being a middle-class wife and mother in Iraq. I would be living in a nice house with electricity, TV, a washing machine, a deep freezer, one or two cars. Perhaps I was in a rut, bored with my routine life with its daily mundane chores.

Then the electricity went off. Not for an hour or a day, but *off* as in bombed out utility plants, blown up government buildings, air fields, highways.

I remember reading an article about what had happened. The women started cooking. They knew the meat would soon rot. They had parties, and invited neighbors. They feasted on meat, overeating as much as they could.

Eventually, they knew they could no longer trust the meat and threw it to the dogs.

And that was the end.

They would have given anything to be in the rut that had been theirs only a week or two earlier — the routine, the predictability, the *boredom*.

We don't have to look so far. Hurricanes and fires have left thousands of Americans without their rut.

In a yoga class, our instructor often reads a passage that says something like this:

"Cherish the ordinariness of life. Savor it. Be grateful for it. Because there are times in our lives when things are anything but ordinary, and we will yearn with all our hearts for an ordinary day."

So I bless my rut. It keeps me steady. I know its curves and dimensions. It frames my life. Yes, there are times to step out of our rut, but also times to simply be grateful that our lives, right now, are stable, calm, predictable, and peaceful.

Indeed we should remember that even when we step out of our rut, if that truly is necessary, we begin to create a new rut. We create patterns and habits, traditions and relationships.

Basically we root ourselves in a new rut.

That doesn't seem so bad.

Sacred

I just had my morning cup of tea — a sacred time for me. When I go to church, I feel an inner hushed joy at the moment of Eucharist. Sacred.

But for others, it is music. Sacred. Nature. Sacred. Gardening. Sacred. Hanging out with the guys at the neighborhood bar. Sacred.

We should never rush past sacred moments, nor take them for granted. They are the sometimes rare moments when *our* inner soul connects directly to the outer world. No meditation, prayer, petitioning required.

We are tuned in, like a radio station, and we pretty much know that the channel will slip off our dial all too soon ... until the next time.

I think we should cultivate the sacred every day. Once we recognize that heart-joy opening to our always busy consciousness, we should take note. *Oh, here is a place where my experience of life feels sacred.*

The nice thing about sacred places and moments is that, generally speaking, they are repeatable.

The sunrise always gives us a lift; our favorite song, that perfect desert, an author we enjoy — all invite us into sacred space. It is not reserved for religion but life itself.

What is the purpose of sacred moments? Why do we have them? What makes them sacred rather than just special?

If we switch just two letters, sacred becomes *scared*. In some respects, the two hover close to each other in real life. We can actually be scared of sacred moments because all our facades collapse in the presence of sacred—we just *are*. Naked to our true self. Even if no one is watching, *we* know that we are unmasked at that moment. Our heart feels a sense of wonder, union, totality.

Sometimes we rush right back out of the sacred because we get scared. We minimize (when we should be maximizing) the time we share with the sacred.

There are, however, two types of sacred: routine and unexpected. The routine includes that cup of tea I love so much.

The unexpected is my short-legged corgi leaping in and out of a mountain of fresh snow. I may be totally engrossed in Brianna's leaps and bounds, or I may be thinking, *I'm freezing. Enough! Let's get back inside!*

So while I recognize that moment of inner joy, of total connection with this sacred sense of being part of something much larger than myself, I am unable to stay in the moment because I'm afraid I'll freeze to death.

Harder yet are those sacred moments of relationship, especially in new encounters. We can sense the sacred between us, but be afraid to hold the eye contact to honor and acknowledge it. We retreat to safe facades: *What do you do? Where do you live?* We are scared of the unexpected sacred. When we should rush towards it, embrace it, acknowledge it, we run away.

The good news is that once the sacred is experienced, we can savor the memory, and often, we can return — more open, more aware.

Sacred, traditionally, seems linked to religion: *You are in a sacred place. Communion is sacred. This is a place of God — it is sacred.*

I would suggest that *sacred* is a matter of the heart, your heart. The goal and purpose of sacred is to connect you directly to Creator/God/Divine Love. We need those moments because so many in our lives feel non-sacred, ordinary, stressful, scary.

When overwhelmed by *those* moments, we can remember that within each of us, there is a sacred channel on our radio. Always there. All we have to do is tune in, and listen.

Thanksgiving

Since today actually *is* Thanksgiving, it must inevitably, perhaps, become my "T" essay. I've been in this small river town in Missouri now for fourteen years. My daughter lives on one coast; my sister on the other. Add to that my reluctance to travel during winter, I could — every year — be home alone.

But small town folk start calling around during the early days of November. "Are you doing anything for Thanksgiving? Come join us." I call these marvelous meals the gathering of the orphans and strays.

For all these years, not one has gone by when we don't somehow coalesce, when we try to make sure everyone has a place to go. Some years are funnier than others. My neighbor Michelene one year decided to serve a Chinese meal, in four courses. As we feasted on one treat after another, she never sat down nor ate, busy getting our next course ready.

On another year, she invited a somewhat homeless, former nun with mental illness to join us. Also at the table was a retired IBM employee with his Russian wife who wore white patent boots, fishnet stockings, a white miniskirt, a tight white top, and a white furry coat. She was also a genius.

The nun refused to eat anything cooked in metal, so Michelene made sure her portion of every course was cooked in ceramic or glassware.

When we sat down to eat, she suggested that our nun offer grace. Suddenly the room was filled with the most exquisite soprano voice, singing praises we had never heard floating on notes never scored on paper. A hush fell over us. She brought thanksgiving, not in a serving dish but in an open heart.

This year, there was an early Thanksgiving at Kara and Stan's. Since they moved to Hannibal, they have taken over the turkey, stuffing, and gravy. The twenty or so who show up bring the rest.

My specialty is a Finnish sweet bread called *pulla* or *nisua*, distinct for its cardamom spice. It takes all day to make. I have to hammer the seeds out of their pods, then grind them to powder. The dough sits, then gets kneaded then rises, rises again, gets formed into three braided loaves, and cooked till still moist, not dry.

I only make it once a year, for obvious reasons.

Sometimes (often) we are really busy on the days leading up to Thanksgiving, including the day itself. Now it has been relegated to hurry-and-eat because Black Friday starts on Thanksgiving Thursday.

Also, there is no guarantee on civility, families being families. Disaffected teenagers, politically opposite relatives, just plain exhaustion all become part of the *dough* of Thanksgiving.

I remember one year sitting with my husband's family when a male member maligned my sister, who at that moment was eating turkey 3,000 miles away. For perhaps one of the few times in my life, I spoke up. "Don't you *ever* talk about my sister like that." Dead silence fell and I did absolutely nothing to stop it. Eventually someone made a benign comment and Thanksgiving life rolled on.

What makes Thanksgiving so amazing, so unique, is that we show up, year after year, traditions firmly in place: the turkey, mashed potatoes, candied yams, creamed peas, pumpkin pie, wine, whiskey, coca cola, coffee, prayer, and a motley assemblage of *us*—as we are, unblemished, at one table.

We somehow express love in its most tattered or glorious clothing.

Recently I saw a double rainbow arching over our town and river, brilliant against a dark and rainy sky. When we sit down at tables, surrounded by our foods and traditions, I can't help but feel there's a rainbow over us.

For this, I give thanks.

Unused

Now this is a lovely word — not yet used, full of potential, dream material, recycling possibilities. there-but-not-yet-seen. I have heard more than once that we actually use very little of our brain. Even more astonishing, I read an article once about a child missing a full half of her (his?) brain, and yet functioning perfectly normally.

I have left unused extraordinarily large portions of my brain — books I have not read, places I have not been, people I have not yet met. There is a whole unused universe out there, just outside my five senses.

I guess the trick is to view, somewhat objectively, what has been unused in our lives, and what we'd like to use before we die. For me, it would be more music, more nature, more awareness, more mystery, and of course, more books. I was raised in a rather heady home, meaning Einstein ranked slightly higher than God (*if,* in my father's mind, God existed at all).

So naturally, I worked hard to excel mentally in a society that actually liked cerebral accomplishments.

Perhaps it was a natural melding of my abilities with what was expected of me, but it meant I truncated other parts of myself rather severely by *not seeing them.*

For example, as children, we are immersed in nature. Our generation played from morning to night, outdoors (told to *stay* outside, preferably all day).

Yet when I went to college, I would never—of my own volition—have joined the university's Trail Club. I went because my older sister liked caving, climbing, hiking, canoeing.

Practically every week-end I hopped into an overcrowded car with my crappy backpack equipment and off we went to somewhere along the Appalachian Trail, West Virginia wildernesses, or on vacations, further afield to the Adirondacks or Acadia National Park.

Even so, I spent more time on the trail *thinking* of things rather than *being* in nature and *observing*.

There was a whole unused universe in a surround-sound setting, and I plowed through it mindlessly.

The same with music.

Our family never listened to it: no radio, no car music system, no purchased stacks of records.

Granted I had a minimalist collection of Elvis and the Beatles, but I also bought the 5-cent specials: *Let's go fishin' instead of just a wishin'*.

I grew up in silence—perfect for reading and becoming even more intellectual!

So today, wanting to explore the unused portions of being a human being at this time on this beautiful planet, I have stepped out of my comfort zone … partially.

My first foray, perhaps not surprisingly, was to explore silence. I meditated. Over time, I found it rich in its own sound. In my best most unexpectedly quiet moments, it felt as rich as a full orchestra reaching a crescendo. (The other times it was quite boring).

Next, I moved into gardening—knowing nothing more than dig-a-hole, insert-plant, and hope. I have never learned the nuances of watering systems, or natural nutrients. Mother Earth has done most of the work in my yard. The hardy thrives; the delicate less so.

Slowly over the years, I think I have developed what has heretofore been unused: relationship with non-human beings. Plants do not "converse" in a human (or even canine or feline) way. But they talk quite vociferously about such things as pests, disease, water.

When things are going well in the garden, who cannot notice the lush foliage, the magnificent tomato, the long-lasting blossom. All of that represented an unused part of me—until I planted a seed, a seedling, a sapling.

Unused does not, to my mind, mean unworthy, unexceptional, unnecessary. It merely means unseen ... yet.

Vision

Vision spans several realms, from the physical to the metaphysical. Apparently there are different ways of seeing. Sometimes we "see" blindly. I remember reading (a long time ago) about a man who had been born blind but because of medical advances could, through surgery, be made to see.

He agreed; the surgery proceeded; he regained his "sight"—but he could not see.

During the initial days, his friends took him to a place to see a lathe for the first time, after years of using it while blind. He had no idea what it was. Finally, he stepped forward and *touched* it. Then he saw.

We now know that during a child's developmental years, the brain must build up the interpretive abilities to *read* and interpret what is seen. Apparently, this is a window that opens, and then closes. If the brain does not build the scaffolding to translate during this time, the person is effectively blind.

More recently I read about a man who had once seen but a chemical burn destroyed his sight when he was about five years old. He too could benefit by medical advances, and he eagerly participated. But seeing simply exhausted him.

Whereas we had developed screening-out filters, he had none. So the chair had as much value as his daughter as the coat he was wearing as the spice on the table. Overwhelmed by sensory input and unable to extract the essential, he too gave up, preferring his blind ability to "see".

Vision, in this scenario, acts as one of our five senses.

At the other extreme, a person may have a vision—a mental leap forward. Ghandi envisioned a new India. For him, that vision felt so concrete and real that he simply lived, totally, within his vision—even though it had not arrived yet.

Then there are those who have near death experiences and they see the other side. Add to them the psychics and mediums, and vision begins to expand way beyond the physical realm.

I suspect all of us see on all of these levels. Often we see unseeingly. We might walk through the woods on a beautiful, sunny fall day, but be talking so intently, we don't see at all. My husband once pointed out that I could not see and talk at the same time. True. I try harder now to see, but when I'm in conversation, it's still hard.

Also, there are moments of insight. A relationship may be tangled up and we get an insight.

Recently, my rescued cat threw up yet again after inhaling his cat food at an almost frenetic rate. Now this has been going on for years, but only yesterday did I get an unexpected insight.

A kitten when I saw him, I scooped his bony body up and carried him home. Once there, I fed him milk and cat food. Like a crazed animal, he couldn't sit still to eat. I watched this abnormal behavior, amazed as he tore around the room, ate, tore around, ate.

Now I understand. I have insight. Even years later, he still worries he'll starve so he gulps his food down; his stomach can't handle it; he throws up.

We are all visionaries, at times. We see something larger than the facts at hand. We step out of the limits of time, space, history, memory. Something clicks into place for us. We have a visionary a-ha.

We are not blind.

We see.

Wizen

Everything over time probably gets wizen. We wither. We shrivel. It doesn't sound very promising. But it's a great word. It has character. Panache. Glaciers wizen. Rocks, through erosion, wizen. We all wizen. It could be a song.

Honestly, a wizened face, filled with cracks and crevices, its smile or frown wrinkles, its missing teeth, lost hair — its *wizen-ness* — has a certain appeal.

First, it proves survival. After all, you can't become wizen in your youth, or your middle age, and really not in your senior years. Wizen belongs to the ancients.

One of our townsmen, about to celebrate his 101st birthday, is showing beginning signs of wizen-ness, though still too spry by far to be a full-fledged member.

Wizen-ness connotes a certain freedom. What on earth do you have to prove any more. You *are*! You are a testament to survival.

It is as though all of life's wisdom starts to shrink in on itself to its very essence. No more long speeches. No more purposes to complete. No lifestyle to defend. Instead, the *value* of life, of love, of experience begins to contract, to draw in.

It is as though the soul, in this human body, begins to dehydrate into its pure essence. That is the nature of wizen-ness.

We see it all around us. In the fall, the trees go into a wizening state. They pull in their sap. They seem bare, dry, corpses in our midst.

Plants are even more dramatic. They shrink into a bulb or a root. Who hasn't put very wizened bulbs into the ground, seeming to seal them forever into death.

As humans, we cannot see the flip side of wizen-ness. It seems to shrink into death, and after death into ash or soil. But that pertains to the physical. The properly wizened soul presumably is the preserve of the afterlife, the other side, heaven, eternity.

I particularly like this word. It seems transitional. To be wizen is to have reached an inner essence of living. I hope we all have encountered someone in this state.

Once, years ago, I "babysat" a man in his mid-eighties while his son and daughter-in-law took a much needed caregiver vacation. After lunch I suggested he sit in the rocking chair in the living room. Then I promptly forgot about him.

My children were elementary school age, and between parenting and cooking, I really forgot all about him, and hours went by.

Around 4:00 PM, I realized with a shock I had paid him no attention whatsoever, and rushed into the living room to see if he needed a snack or a drink, or just conversation.

I approached him, and he looked up at me and said, "The sun feels so good on my feet."

That is wizen-ness.

X   marks the spot

Any of us can examine our life and find Xs that mark turning points. Sometimes we come to a full stop, sometimes a semi-colon where we pause, sometimes a ... meaning we haven't a clue what to do next, and sometimes a colon or dash—moving forward confidently into new territory.

We punctuate our lives with major (and sometimes seemingly minor) events. Of course, our birth is an exclamation point, for ourselves, and those to whom our care is entrusted.

Xs can also be kind of a burial ground. We place what we consider to be errors of judgment, action or inaction, missteps and mishaps, into a kind of psychic cemetery, which we visit once in a while.

We remember; we may place flowers of forgiveness on the graves of our transgressions; and hopefully, we move on until the next X occurs.

Xs can also be a kind of cathedral, a sacred shrine of remembered moments in our lives when things went well: we got married; we raised children; we served our community; we enjoyed our work; we aged gracefully.

We can enter these X-sites in our cathedral, and sit with them in happy memory.

It seems to me that X-marks-the-spot moments, the high and low points of our life, enrich us tremendously. They have value. For one thing, they express poignantly that we have lived.

I remember going on a retreat with our church staff one year. One of our "experiences" was to draw a map of our lives—who and what had influenced us.

Mine was quietly modest, perhaps because I was still rather young. But I waited with curiosity to see what our minister might have drawn.

He held up his map of life, and it was crammed with stick-figures of men and women- too many to count. *People* had blessed his life. His four brothers, his deep relationships with parishioners, his fellow ministers made his life feel complete and whole and blessed.

His life was X-full. And I think at that moment we all realized our lives were X-full. He had simply seen it and named it and called our attention to it.

He didn't see an X-filled life as one comprised of major victories.

He didn't count job advancements, accolades, recognition at all on his chart-of-life. He counted his relationships with *people* – the love that flowed between them, the sense of community intertwined in fellowship, the joy of simply helping one another to get through the day.

Xs, if we see our life as a glass half full rather than half empty, will mark the spots of our life as well lived. We learned; we loved; we shared.

X-marks-our-spot.

Yes

We all probably ought to say yes more often. Our no's are usually couched in fear. Personally, I've found my yes's getting a bit fewer. I have lots of reasons, mostly physical. Especially travel. Even the thought of suitcases, pet care, airports, time changes, makes me want to run to my recliner and read a good book.

So my yes's get a bit harder with age. I talk to myself about that. *You can do this. Really.*

My daughter got married last year. As preparations, ideas, and timetables swirled into nightmarish proportions, I said to myself, *She needs a 40-year-old mom.*

So I gave her one ... myself, the way I had been 30 years ago.

I cut ribbons, painted boards, chopped apples, ran errands, packed boxes, washed dishes. Then I came home and tanked for about a month.

That was a fun *yes*. And worth every ounce of energy extracted from me. I actually felt young again. Recharged with remembering how I once zipped through life.

Now I see yes's I'd love to do, but I hesitate. Hike through England. Yes. Drive cross country again. Yes. Visit national parks. Yes. Oh, and fall in love again. YES.

Technically I could do all of them (except making love crash into my life), but the exhaustion factor keeps rising. Not to mention what it takes to "maintain" myself.

My yes's take more the form of a daily to-do list. Yes to exercise, vitamins, house cleaning, writing, weaving, reading, socializing, walking the dog, giving the bird his meds. Then the day is gone. Poof.

True, a lot of yes's but not exactly inspiring.

I believe there is an unexplored world of yes that I haven't noticed.

Doing a house trade for three months, so I can take my dog, cat, and bird with me. Seriously volunteering, as in a one-year full-time commitment. Do a Spanish language immersion for three weeks somewhere.

When we were younger, we tossed out yes's like cheap confetti. "Want to go on a 50-mile hike?" Sure, no problem, when? Want to travel overseas for three months, camping-style? Absolutely. Do you mind working 60 hours a week? Sounds like fun. I can do it.

And multi-tasking! The scourge of the yes'ers. Most of us honestly pack way too many yes's into a day. We want to be agreeable, responsible, sociable.

We want to prove we can do it.

A lot (too many) women are succumbing to work fatigue in their 30s. Fibromyalgia. Chronic Fatigue Syndrome. Adrenal Exhaustion. Irritable Bowel Syndrome.

The root of the problem is actually a Yes-Imbalance. We have yes'd ourselves into a pit. Now we have to yes our way out.

There is a difference between an obligatory yes (yes, I'll raise my kids) to an optional yes (I'll take them to soccer, basketball, ballet, drama … they need to have an enriching life).

When actively parenting, I loved the day when one of my kids would come into the kitchen and say, "I'm BORED." I'd say, "That's *great*." Not finding any relief from me, they had to dig for their own yes. Yes to drawing or yes to reading or yes to bicycling or yes to calling a friend and hanging out.

Yes, taken in balanced portions, opens the whole wide world to us.

YES!

Zany

I remember walking one day down to the Hannibal dock where our Mississippi River-loving visitors tied up their boats.

The usual motorboats, large and small, filled the spaces. Amid this well-groomed fleet floated a homemade raft made of pallets.

At every corner, the owner had nailed a lengthy 2x4, from which hung a myriad of belongings, from plastic gallon jugs to tarps, ropes, clothing. pots.

Apparently the owner planned to pole his way from Minnesota to New Orleans but started out a tad too late. He arrived in Hannibal mid-November. Tying up his craft-of-sorts, he headed for our only coffee shop, Java Jive.

Within the hour, he had found a wintertime sofa to live upon, a menial wages job, and a town to live in ... for a couple of years.

I loved that raft, that derelict piece of junk, proudly perched in our Mark-Twain-made-famous town.

No, he didn't sail off in spring. He probably dragged it off to Bear Creek and sank it, or left it on an island somewhere.

The river periodically drops zany members of our society into our somewhat staid town.

One year a troupe of college students puttered into town, tying up at the same dock. They proceeded to swarm our town, plastering posters everywhere promising a performance at Nipper Park.

We, the bored denizens of Hannibal, showed up en masse with our lawn chairs to be stupefied by an incredibly bad performance of non-singers, non-dancers, non-jugglers, and seriously bad storytellers.

Then, they passed the hat and we enthusiastically obliged, sending this unwashed (and I mean *literally* unwashed) mass of youth downstream.

These zany moments keep a basically conservative midwest town from ever taking itself too seriously.

I have often considered us a prime site for a sitcom somewhat like *Northern Exposure* (for those who remember that whacko comedy based in a small one-bar town in Alaska).

We've had haute couture by a Russian immigrant who offered us runway shows followed by borscht. We've had a slightly off-balance nun who prayed for us in a beautiful soprano voice.

We have street minstrels from guitar to sax and harmonica, wooing us with everything from country to classical to gospel.

Hannibal, because of Mark Twain, has grown up on zany. His humor permeated our streets even though he left after completing his childhood. He lingered awhile as a riverboat pilot, but then exited west, then east, then Europe, then world. He'd come back a couple of times. Once he stood on the grand staircase at Rockcliffe Manor giving a talk to the citizens.

Decades later, cross-dressing transvestites descended that same staircase, offering a fabulous evening of Broadway-style entertainment with way too much pot smoke drifting up.

We have been told we live near one of earth's vortexes, meaning we are spiritually enhanced, and attract kindred folk. We have an excellent young medium raising her family in our town, and we have embraced her wholeheartedly.

Zany is not deranged, or mentally ill (though some of us are). Zany sees life through the best lens possible, with Humor:

… often unrealized by the owner, but spectacularly recognized by everyone else … and highly approved.

Made in the USA
Columbia, SC
30 April 2019